The E

Other books by Peter Eldin in Armada

THE TRICKSTER'S HANDBOOK ✓

THE SECRET AGENT'S HANDBOOK ✓

THE WHIZZKID'S HANDBOOK

TOP OF THE POPS QUIZ

ISN'T THAT AMAZING!

THE NEW ARMADA TV QUIZ BOOK

Peter Eldin

The Explorer's Handbook

with drawings by Roger Smith

An Armada Original

The Explorer's Handbook was first published in
Armada in 1980 by Fontana Paperbacks,
14 St. James's Place, London SW1A 1PS.

© Eldin Editorial Services 1980.

Printed in Great Britain by
Richard Clay (The Chaucer Press) Ltd,
Bungay, Suffolk

Contents

Introduction

Deep in the African jungle the great explorer Dr Deadstone is lost. Does he panic? No! Does he shout for help? No! What does he do? He just opens his knapsack and removes his copy of *The Explorer's Handbook* which gives him valuable hints on how to set up camp, how to escape from attacking animals, and how to find his way home to his mummy.

Across the other side of the world the famous Arctic explorer Jack Frost has crashed his aeroplane miles from civilisation. Does he panic? No! Does he shout for help? No! What does he do? He just delves into his fur-lined boots and brings forth a frozen copy of *The Explorer's Handbook* to find out how to build an igloo and how to construct a signal that searching aircraft will spot.

Any explorer, whether he be canoeing up the treacherous River Ouse in search of the lost city of Bedford, climbing up the Himalayas to try Sherpa Ea Ting's tasty Mongolian munch, or camping in the Rainy Day Tenting Park in the wilds of inhospitable Knotty Ash, should carry a copy of *The Explorer's Handbook* with him. If all else fails it can always be burned to provide a signal fire.

But before setting light to this valuable work, just consider the fact that it contains many useful tips which will provide you with trouble-free exploring, show you how to

find your way when the compass goes on strike, tell you how to make Red Indian hand signals for communicating with friendly natives, how to leave messages for other members of your expedition, and even how to forecast what the weather is going to be like.

And when you are resting from your intrepid adventures and trans-global travels you will still need a copy of *The Explorer's Handbook* by your side, as it also contains a few puzzles over which you can ponder whilst waiting for the next canoe up the Orinoco.

In short, this book contains everything Dr Livingstone should have known before he ventured into the unknown regions of darkest Clapham Common. No explorer should be without it.

Try camping in your own garden..

Planning an Expedition

If you have never been on an expedition into unexplored territory before, it is a good idea to practise as much as you can before you go. Practise putting your tent up until you can do it without making a fool of yourself. Then spend a night or two in the tent. Even in your own garden, camping can be quite an adventure – provided you ignore the worried look of your mother as she peeps through the windows of the house every ten minutes or so to make sure you are all right.

Once you have tried a few sessions in the garden you can go a little further afield. For the first expedition do not go more than half an hour's walking distance from your home or that of a friend. This may be a bit of a problem if you live in the middle of a large town such as London or Birmingham. Camping in the centre of Piccadilly Circus or the Bull Ring is not to be recommended!

If there is not a suitable place near you then you will have to go further away – but make sure that you are reasonably close to civilisation. Then, if you get into trouble through inexperience, or you suddenly find you have forgotten to pack the peanuts, you can always get help easily. In this way you will learn what things you will need on a longer and more distant exploration.

For your first expeditions try to borrow equipment from friends and relatives. You can then find out whether or not you really like exploring before you start buying equipment of your own.

All expeditions require advance planning if they are to be successful. It is no good taking lots of tinned foods only to discover that you have forgotten to pack a tin opener. Several weeks before your expedition make out a list of all the things you need. A sample list is given on the next page. You will also find specimen lists of first aid and survival items on pages 41 and 29.

Many modern explorers carry their equipment by hovercraft, helicopter, or Land Rover. They can therefore take with them all the home comforts available. But if you are exploring wild territory, modern forms of transport may not be suitable. You must therefore consider the weight of the things you are taking. If you are planning a hiking or cycling expedition and you cannot afford to employ numerous native bearers or pack horses you will find that this question of weight can be most important. So, when you have made your list you may find it worthwhile to go through it again and cross out all the things you do not really need.

Firstly consider the weight of the things you are taking...

Expedition Checklist

The things that you have to take with you when you go exploring will depend to a large extent on the area that you will be visiting and the time of the year that your expedition is to take place. There is, for example, little point in taking sun tan lotion if you are trekking through the wastelands of snowy Siberia, or of packing large woolly jumpers if you are crossing the Australian desert. The list given on this page is just a guide to some of the things you may need to include when you make out your own check-list.

Clothing
> change of underwear
> change of socks
> walking shoes/boots
> raincoat/anorak (a light one)
> bathing costume
> pyjamas
> sleeping bag

Eating
> food (see page 15)
> unbreakable plate and mug
> cutlery
> tin opener
> cooking pot
> washing-up liquid
> tea towels
> water container
> cooking foil

DON'T FORGET
THE CHANGE OF SOCKS!!!!

Toiletries
- soap
- towel
- toothbrush
- toothpaste
- face cloth
- mirror
- comb
- toilet paper

Other items
- compass
- maps
- clock or watch
- matches
- penknife
- first aid kit (see page 41)
- emergency kit (see page 29)
- emergency food kit (see page 31)

Food, Glorious Food

When considering what food to take with you on your expedition remember that you have got to carry it. Try to take items that can be easily prepared but bear in mind that you will want a change of diet. It is, however, quite possible to devise a list of foods that you like that will provide you with variety and yet be easy to prepare. Cooking utensils are heavy, so try to restrict their use as much as possible.

Before drawing up your food list take a look in your local trading post. You will find that there are a great number of convenience foods to which you need only add hot water to provide a nourishing meal. These are the ones to take with you on your expedition. You will be surprised at the great variety that is available.

There are of course many foods that can be obtained in tins that have only to be heated to provide a meal. But the trouble with tins is that they are heavy. They are also rather awkward to dispose of.

If possible, try to take some fresh foods with you. Again there are disadvantages. They are bulky and they may not last for long. You may, however, find that you have camped near a trading post where you can obtain fresh supplies and this will save you having to carry a great deal with you.

Bear in mind you will want a change of diet...

15

Always bear in mind the length of time you can keep various foods before they become inedible. Fresh food such as meat, fish, and milk should really be eaten on the day they are bought. Sausages and bacon can be kept for a few days as they contain preservative. Foods that can be kept for a longer period of up to one week include eggs, cheese, fruit, and vegetables.

Some food will keep more or less indefinitely. This includes all tinned products and dehydrated foods. Coffee and tea will also keep for a long time provided that their containers are sealed after use. If taking cereals or other food that comes in boxes remove them from the box and carry them in sealed plastic bags. The boxes will only take up too much room and add to the rubbish you have to get rid of.

Try to vary your diet as much as you can during your expedition and remember that fresh foods are better for you than processed foods. If, however, you think that a particular food has gone off or you think it is in any way doubtful, always throw it out and don't eat it.

Fantastic Food Facts

As you travel around the world on your explorations you will discover many strange and curious customs concerning food. Here are some that you are likely to encounter as you travel around the world:

A favourite delicacy of the Fiji Islanders is Kava. This is a drink made from the roots of a type of pepper plant. Drinking kava is an important ceremonial occasion. The person of highest rank takes the first drink of the intoxicating liquid and it is not long before most of the people taking part in the ceremony are very drunk indeed.

In Japan you could be offered fugu. This is made from puffer fish, which sounds fine until you realise that puffer fish is extremely poisonous! Special training has to be given to Japanese chefs before they are allowed to serve fugu. This training is to ensure that all the poison is removed before the fish is cooked. But, nevertheless, a large number of people die each year in Japan as a result of tasting a tempting morsel of fugu.

In some parts of Africa and Asia it is believed that men, particularly during wartime, will become weak if their food is prepared by women. So, if you intend to go into battle don't let your mum cook the dinner!

In Fiji, people eat shark flesh, but they are not allowed to eat the dorsal fin – this and the head of the fish is always reserved for the chief of the tribe.

Grub for the Australian aborigine consists of grubs! Larvae of various species of grubs are very popular but the all-time favourite is the large yellow wichity grub. Ugh!

On the Map

If your expedition takes you through areas that have been mapped by previous explorers then it is well worthwhile taking copies of the maps with you. A good map will give you a great deal of information about the place you are visiting. Many of the features on the map will be represented by symbols and there should be a table of these symbols to tell you what each one means.

When using a map, hold it so the details on it face the same way you are facing. The map itself may be upside down or held at an angle but you will find it easier to compare with the features around you. To find your position using a map you must first look for some outstanding landmarks. Now try to find the same landmarks on the map. Hold the map out in front of you so the position of the landmarks correspond with their positions on the map. Now draw imaginary lines from the real landmarks and through the map landmarks. The point at which these imaginary lines meet is your position.

If there are no recognisable landmarks visible place your compass on the map so that the needle and the direction of the map (which will be indicated) are both pointing north. Even in areas where there are few definable features, such as deserts or mountainous terrain, this procedure will help you to decide in what direction you should be moving. Once you know which way you are facing you can begin to make some attempt to identify what is around you.

It is as well to do this checking as often as possible during an expedition. If you are in the desert and a sandstorm blows up or in the Arctic when a blizzard starts, or in the jungle where it becomes particularly dense you will always have some idea of your location as a result of your last check.

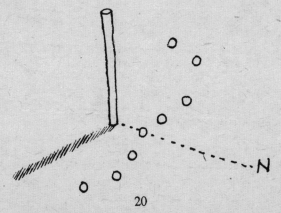

Points to Ponder

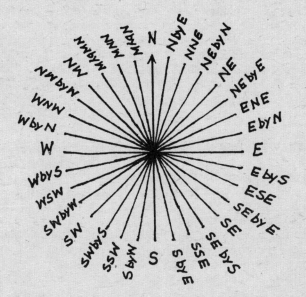

A compass is used by explorers to find the direction of north, and from this the directions of south, east, and west. It is essential equipment when undertaking expeditions in unfamiliar territory.

There are four main (cardinal) points of direction and even non-explorers should know them and their relationship to one another. They are north (N), south (S), east (E), and west (W). Between the cardinal points are four intermediate points. These are north-east (NE), south-east (SE), north-west (NW), and south-west (SW).

For most explorers it is sufficient to know just these eight points but they can be subdivided again to provide sixteen points. The additional eight points are north north-east, east north-east, east south-east, and so on. By subdividing yet again, to add north by east, north-east by east, east by south, and so on, thirty-two points are obtained.

Naming the thirty-two points of the compass in the correct order starting from north and going clockwise around the compass is known as "boxing the compass". At first sight this might appear to be rather a useless accomplishment but it will enable the explorer to get thoroughly acquainted with the compass and this could prove extremely useful. Why don't you have a go at learning all the points as shown on the illustration. It is not really so difficult as it sounds.

Crazy Compass

No matter where in the world you decide to explore, you should always take this compass along with you. It never fails.

To make it, all you need is a piece of card and a pencil. Cut the card into the shape shown in the illustration. Mark one of the arrows with the letter N to represent north. Mark the other arrow head with S for south.

To find which way is north using this compass all you have to do is place it down so that the S end is pointing to the south. The other end is now pointing to the north!

Boxing the compass...

Make Your Own Compass

For serious expeditions you should take the best compass you can afford. But for practice and for fun it is worth-while making your own compass. It is quite easy to do.

First trace the compass shown on page 21 on to a sheet of card. Do not bother with all thirty-two points. The eight main points will be sufficient.

Now take a strip of thin steel and rub it repeatedly with one end of a bar magnet. The rubbing must be done in the same direction each time. Eventually the steel strip will become sufficiently magnetised to act as a compass needle. If you cannot find a suitable strip of steel you could use an old razor blade, but do make sure it is blunt.

Fix the strip to a piece of cork using modelling cement or a waterproof glue. If all else fails, you could use a drawing pin to attach the metal to the cork. The piece of cork should be just large enough to support the metal strip when placed in water.

When you float it in water the metal strip will float around until it is pointing north and south. Find out which end is pointing north and mark it with a large letter N.

To the Wild West

There are two ways you can use this magnetic pointer and your compass card when out exploring. The first requires the use of a glass-bottomed container, such as a jam jar or a shallow bowl. Put some water in the bowl and float the pointer in it. Now slide the card under the bowl so that north on the card is directly below the N on the pointer. By looking through the bottom of the bowl at the compass card you can read off any direction.

If you do not have a glass-bottomed bowl, do not despair. Use any other dish or bowl and simply place the card alongside it so that north on the card and the N on the pointer are in the same position.

If you learn the various points of the compass you can do away with the card completely, for once you know the direction of north you will know all the other directions.

Stick Compass

This is a useful means of finding the direction of north when you are exploring. The sun must be shining and you must start the procedure before mid-day. All you have to do is to push a stick into the ground. Now place a stone at the end of the stick's shadow. As the day goes on the shadow will move. Keep putting stones at the end of the shadow at regular intervals, say every five or ten minutes. As noon approaches you will notice the shadow getting shorter and shorter. After mid-day the shadow will begin to grow longer again and you can stop putting the stones down.

Now look for the stone that is closest to the stick. That indicates the shortest shadow and it will have been placed there at about mid-day. A line drawn from the stick to the stone will point due north.

Sense of Site

Here are a few points you should bear in mind when choosing a site in which to make camp.

If you set up camp on private land always ask the owner for permission. Sometimes you may be asked to pay a fee. Farmers will often allow you to camp on their land without charge. (In many cases you will find that although the farmer does not charge, the bull that lives in the field will charge you later.)

You may wake up
with a cow in
your tent...

Never pitch your tent in a dried-up river bed. If it rains that river bed may not be dry for long and your whole expedition could be washed away.

Try to avoid fields in which cattle are liable to graze. You may end up next morning with a cow in your tent. Elephant trails should be avoided for the same reason.

Try to set up your camp near to a convenient water supply. Never try to copy the Irish sea scout who tried to pitch his tent whilst he was still at sea.

Try to pitch your camp on level ground. It may be funny to see someone sliding downhill out of their tent during the middle of the night but the person concerned may not be so amused.

It is a good idea to keep clear of trees. This is especially important if there is any likelihood of a thunderstorm. No one wants a fully grown tree or a branch crashing through their tent after being hit by lightning. Even in wet weather, without the lightning, camping beneath trees is not recommended as water will continue to drop on your tent well after the rain has stopped. In winter there may be a danger of falling branches. Camping under trees in the summer months is not quite so hazardous and the trees can provide welcome shelter from both sun and wind. It is always a good idea to camp *near* trees, however, as this will provide you with a constant supply of wood for your camp fire.

Look at the nearby trees and see which way they lean. This will give you an indication of the general direction of the wind. Pitch your tent so that the wind will not blow you back into the tent every time you open the flap.

Clear up your rubbish. Do not leave it around where it could endanger animals. Burn what you can and keep the rest in a polythene bag. This can either be buried or taken with you to a place where it can be disposed of. Empty tin cans take up less room in the rubbish bag if they are first flattened by treading on them.

The smell can be quite overpowering...

Make sure the area in which you are to pitch your tent is clean, free from nettles and ant hills, and that it does not contain any exposed stones.

Dig a small channel around your tent to carry away rain water.

Avoid a camp site that is downwind from farm buildings housing animals. You could find the smell quite over-powering.

Avoid marshy areas or stagnant water as these attract insects and you could end up being bitten.

Butter and milk can be kept fresh by putting them in a polythene bag and suspending this in a stream. But make sure the bag is tied securely or your rations may float away.

Empty tins take up less room if they are flattened

Thank you

Survival Kit

Survival is a serious business. Whether you are exploring the snowy wastes of Siberia, the jungles of South America, or the arid wastes of Newcastle-upon-Tyne, you will find it useful to have some knowledge of the basic techniques that will ensure your survival should anything go wrong.

Many survival techniques are described in this book. In addition to knowing something of these techniques, all explorers should carry a survival kit – a collection of items that will help you to survive in an emergency.

A basic survival kit to be carried on all expeditions should include:

> a first aid kit (see page 41)
> survival food kit (see page 31)
> a copy of *The Explorer's Handbook*
> a compass
> a whistle
> a penknife
> a box of matches
> a candle
> a plastic sheet

It may also prove useful to include a lightweight torch.

All of these items could be wrapped in the plastic sheet and tied with a long length of rope – something else that could prove very useful in an emergency.

Instead of plastic sheeting it is better to carry a large plastic bag. It can always be split open to form a large sheet if required. As a bag it will be found particularly useful if one of the party suffers from shock, a normal occurrence in all but the most minor of injuries. Put the body, *but not the head,* of the patient into the bag and this will help him to remain warm and relaxed. The plastic bag will also act as a handy sleeping bag should you need one. But once again, care should be taken to keep the bag away from the head.

29

A plastic bag will also come in handy to carry all your dirty washing home to mother!

BASIC SURVIVAL KIT To be carried on all expeditions . . . .

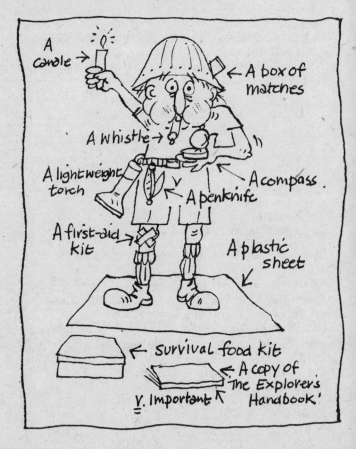

A candle →

← A box of matches

A whistle →

A lightweight torch

A compass

A penknife

A first-aid kit

A plastic sheet

← Survival food kit

← A copy of 'The Explorer's Handbook!'

V. Important →

Survival Food Kit

In addition to your normal food supplies it is well worth taking along a special survival food kit just in case anything goes wrong – although even in an emergency situation it will be a while before your food supplies run out. On top of that you would be surprised how long you can survive without food (although you will not last for very long without water).

The food can be put in with your other survival equipment or in a special tin of its own. The basic rule in deciding what items to include is that they should be light, compact, and energy-giving.

Suitable items are:
    dates (or dried fruits such as raisins)
    chocolate
    glucose or sugar cubes
    biscuits
    peanuts
    beef stock cubes

How about a date?

None of these will take up much room in your survival food kit but they are all things that your body can quickly and easily convert into energy. The beef stock cubes will also provide a hot, tasty, and cheering drink that will warm you up and make you feel less tired.

It is possible to add many more items to this list but that would defeat the whole object. You would probably end up carrying more food in your survival kit than you had in your everyday supplies!

Survival in a Fountain Pen

During the Second World War, air crews often carried fountain pens that were not fountain pens at all. They were survival kits. Inside the pen were pep pills, a compass, a map, and other items to ensure the man's survival.

You could make up a similar survival kit yourself with a bit of thought. First get an old fountain pen – the fatter it is the better. Remove all the works and give it a good wash out.

Now let's see what we could get in it:

Some matches would be useful, but in order to save space break them in half. Wax them as described on page 61 to make sure they do not get damp. Magnetise a pin and put that in the pen. Such a pin will always point to the north when floated in water so it could prove very useful. Roll up a piece of tin foil and put this into the pen. This will be useful as a signal flasher as described on page 101. It might be a good idea to wrap the foil around the matches to give them further protection from the damp. A small safety pin will probably fit into the pen and so will a small candle saved from your last birthday cake.

If you still have some room you could pour sugar into the pen to fill the gaps. This could provide you with a useful source of energy in an emergency.

See if you can think of anything else that would fit into the pen and which could be of assistance to you.

Sticks and Stones

It is sometimes useful to leave messages for other members of your expedition who may be following your route. As the natives may be unfriendly head hunters it is a good idea to leave signs that your friends will understand but which will not mean anything to anyone else. The best way to do this is to make your signs with natural materials such as sticks and stones. Here are some signs you may find useful. If you need to leave any other messages, make them up with your friends before you start out into unknown territory and you will have a signalling system that only you will know.

These signs will also prove useful in your camp, for if the rest of the party is away and you have to leave camp for some reason you can let them know where you have gone.

STICKS AND STONES

Go this way.

Do not go this way.

Not far to go.

Start from here.

Go back.

I've gone home

We are lost
We have been eaten by crocodiles
Airport ahead...
The natives are unfriendly
Grrr.
Grrr...

Tanning Your Hide

One way explorers use to let everyone know they have had a successful expedition is to get themselves a glorious sun tan. There is nothing wrong in this but a lot of explorers go about it the wrong way and end up with burned and peeling skin. Here is how you can get yourself a tan without being burned.

All you have to do is take things gradually. Unless you are a keen outdoor type it is quite likely that your body has not been exposed to the elements for some time. You must then bear in mind that your body will not be used to the sun. It is very tempting to rush out and sunbathe at the first sign of the sun, but don't. If you want to tan without burning, make your first sunbathing session a very short one. Perhaps as little as fifteen minutes. On subsequent days of your expedition you can gradually increase the time you spend in the sun.

If you are lucky enough to mount an expedition to a really sunny place you should spend the first couple of days fully dressed. This will get parts of your skin used to the hot sun before you start to sunbathe. Some parts of your body are more sensitive to sun than others. These are your nose, shoulders, knees, tops of your feet, and the backs of your legs. It is therefore a good idea to cover up these parts while sunbathing and expose them to the sun for shorter periods than for the rest of your body. Whenever you go out in strong sun always wear a hat and keep the back of your neck covered.

Do not think it is "soppy" to use a sun tan oil. It can help to protect your skin. There are lots of sun tan lotions, oils, and creams on the market. Before you go on your epic exploration ask your local witch doctor which will be the best one for you to use. If you have a fair skin you will need more protection than someone with a darker skin.

One thing to be wary of is a breeze. If there is a breeze you may not think it is very hot. Because of this you may think you can ignore the rules. You can't. You will burn just as much on a breezy day as you will on a calm day — so watch out. You could be toasted to a crisp before you realise it.

All of this, of course, depends upon the sun shining sufficiently brightly to give you a tan. If it is not too strong or if your expedition is to the rain forests of Wigan you can stay out for much longer periods.

You can even get suntanned on a cloudy day, as the ultra-violet rays that cause your skin to burn go through the clouds. It is not, however, recommended that you go sunbathing when it is raining. You may turn a lovely golden brown but it will not be a tan. It will be rust!

frizzle
frizzle

Escape From Animals

Sooner or later during your explorations you will probably encounter a wild animal that does not particularly like you (except as food). There are various tactics you can adopt to get you out of any tricky situation but these techniques vary from animal to animal. The tips given below will give you some idea of what you can do to escape from any wild animal that you may encounter:

Elephant. Always carry a telephone in your emergency kit. When an elephant charges, all you have to do is to pick up the receiver and say, "It's for you." With a bit of luck the elephant will stop charging and take the receiver from you for, as everyone knows, no elephant can resist a trunk call.

(It's a reversed charge call)

Rhinoceros. Should a rhinoceros charge at you there is very little you can do except panic. Some explorers do, however, take along with them a team of bricklayers to cope with just such an emergency. All you have to do is to keep the rhinoceros occupied while your team of bricklayers build a thick brick wall. As soon as this is done you stand in front of it. The rhino charges and at the last possible moment you step aside so that the horned attacker plunges straight into the wall. You will have escaped from the danger and the rhinoceros will have quite a headache the following day.

Abominable Snowman. If you are exploring in the Himalayas it is quite possible that you will come across the dreaded Abominable Snowman. If this happens there is only one thing you can try – light a match and with a bit of luck the Abominable Snowman will melt.

Tiger. To escape from a man-eating tiger is really quite simple. All you have to do is to call him "sergeant". As he has many more stripes than a sergeant he will stop to argue with you. This should give you ample opportunity to make your escape.

Laughing Jackass. Should you ever be attacked by a laughing jackass all you have to do is laugh. He will think that you are one of the family and will not bother to attack. If you can convince him that you are his mother-in-law he is very likely to run away.

Polar Bear. The best way to prevent a polar bear from attacking you is to take all your clothes off. All big bears like little bears – and with your clothes off you will certainly be a little bare, so the polar bear will ignore you.

Zebra. On the whole, zebras are fairly docile animals. They are too busy crossing roads to bother attacking explorers. However, should one charge you, the best defence is to ask it one simple question: "Are you black with white stripes or white with black stripes?" That should get him very confused and while he is trying to work out the answer you can slip quietly away.

Leopard. In your emergency kit you should always carry an aerosol dye remover. This will prove invaluable when a leopard attacks. Squirt the spray at the leopard – that should knock the spots off him.

Gorilla. The best form of defence when a gorilla attacks is to act crazy – for everyone knows that gorillas cannot resist nuts.

39

Exploring Enigmas

There may be times during your expedition when you will have time to relax. While you are resting in front of the camp fire or you are waiting for the next mule train up the Khyber Pass, try solving some of these puzzles.

The Two Explorers
Two explorers are pitching camp alongside the River Nile. One explorer is the father of the other explorer's son. How then are the two explorers related?

The Long Walk
The great Polar explorer S. Keemo set out from the North Pole and walked ten miles south. Then he turned and walked ten miles west. Once again he turned and walked ten miles north. He then stopped and set up camp. How far from the North Pole was he at that point?

Burial Party
A party of explorers were canoeing along the River Ungabi which flows along the border between Lendar and Inbopoland. Half of the party were Lendarese and the other half were Inbopomen. Suddenly the canoes went over a terrible waterfall. As they were on the border between the two countries would the survivors of the disaster be buried in Lendar or Inbopo?

Polar Bears and Penguins
Why do polar bears never eat penguins?

The Chase
In an attempt to escape from a tribe of angry natives, an explorer rushed from the village clearing and into the jungle. How far into the jungle could the natives follow the explorer?

Answers on page 127

First Aid Kit

All expeditions should carry some first aid equipment. This should be kept together in a tin box. It is possible to buy such boxes already fully equipped but you can make a kit yourself quite easily.

Get a tin box measuring about eight inches by six inches. The box should have a tight-fitting lid. Wash the box out thoroughly and make sure that it is completely dry before you put any first aid materials into it.

Do not put every medical item you can possibly think of into the tin. Keep it light and simple. The items that are essential and which should be in every first aid box are as follows:

> several squares of lint
> plasters
> two or three bandages of different widths
> two safety pins
> aspirins
> small pair of scissors
> tube of antiseptic cream
> small bottle of vinegar
> small packet of bicarbonate of soda

If you have got room it is also useful to put a St. John's Ambulance man in the first aid kit. Failing this you will find it useful to include a small booklet on basic first aid. (If there is room you could even include books on second aid, third aid, and perhaps lemon-ade.)

THIRST AID KIT →

First Aid

Generally speaking, the object of first aid treatment is not to cure the patient but simply to prevent matters from getting worse until a doctor can be consulted. To this end there are a number of things that every explorer should know. It is not necessary to be a trained doctor to know what you should do in an emergency.

First aid is not intended as a substitute for a doctor. It is simply a means of coping with the situation as best you can until you can contact a doctor.

Speed of action is an essential of any first aid treatment. It is no good trying to learn first aid when an emergency situation arises. It is too late then. All explorers owe it to themselves and to the rest of their party to have some knowledge of basic first aid before they go out on an expedition.

If the patient has been badly injured it is as well not to move him unless absolutely necessary. If you are caught in the middle of an avalanche, or it is pouring with rain, or there are any other reasons why the patient could be further injured by remaining where he is, then you must of course move him to safety. But in doing this be as careful as you can. In moving an injured person great care must be taken to support any limbs that could be broken. Moving someone in such a state can be extremely bad for the patient so, as said before, do not move an injured person unless it is absolutely necessary.

Before any form of treatment make sure that the patient is warm and comfortable. Loosen any tight clothing around the neck and the chest. Unless you have been trained in first aid do not attempt to treat anything that could be serious.

Using Bandages
The purpose of a bandage is to hold a dressing in place, to prevent a limb from being moved, to provide support for a limb, and to stop bleeding. There are two principal types

42

of bandage – the triangular bandage and the roller bandage. The triangular bandage can be formed into a roller bandage if required, by simply folding the top edge down several times.

It is a good idea to practise bandaging different parts of the body. Get together with a fellow explorer and take it in turns to bandage one another up for imaginary wounds. Alternatively, you could practise on a smaller brother or sister – it might be a good way of keeping them quiet for a few minutes.

The illustrations will give you an idea of how various bandages should be applied.

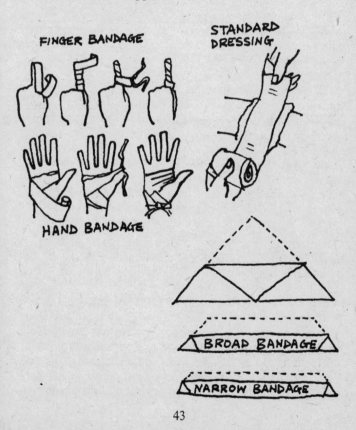

Coat Stretcher

Although you should never move an injured person, there may be occasions when you have to and you do not have a stretcher available. An improvised stretcher can be made from two coats and two poles.

Turn the coats inside-out and do them up with the sleeves inside. Now push two sturdy poles through the sleeves and the stretcher is complete.

Always test this stretcher before putting the injured person on it.

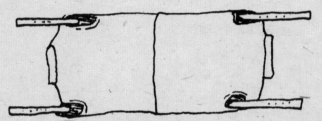

COAT STRETCHER

N.B The Two coats are turned inside-out

Human Carriers

There are several ways you can move an injured person from one place to another. Some are described here but remember that you can often do more harm than good moving someone who is injured. Never move someone unless their injuries are slight or if it is absolutely necessary.

If the injured person has hurt a leg and can get along with some support, you can become a human crutch. Hold the patient's arm around your neck. Your other arm grasps his clothing at the far side. Most of the weight is taken on your shoulders. If necessary, the injured person could carry a sturdy stick in his free hand to provide additional support.

HUMAN
CRUTCH

The fireman's lift can be used on occasion. Place your right arm through the patient's legs. Take his right hand in your left as you crouch down and place the top of your back against his chest. Lift the person up on to the top of your back. Transfer his right hand to your right hand.

This lift should never be used on anyone who is a great deal heavier than you or you will be the one who is injured.

If two people are available to carry a third, they can use the four-handed seat. Face the other person and grasp your left wrist with your right hand. The other person does the same. Now clasp the other helper's right wrist with your left hand. The helper does the same so that a strong bridge is formed with the arms.

Both helpers now crouch down so that the patient can sit on the seat so formed. He puts his arms around the shoulders of the supporters to provide additional support.

If the patient is unable to put his arms around the helpers' shoulders as in the four-handed seat, then the helpers must use one hand each to support the patient. In this case they would form a two-handed seat in which they grasp hands by placing their fingers into the other person's hand. It is a good idea to have a handkerchief between the hands to prevent your nails digging into one another.

FOUR HANDED SEAT

FOUR HANDED SEAT

Nature's Way

Explorers occasionally get lost. When they do, they rely upon their compass to get them back home safely. But what happens if they lose their compass? Well, believe it or not, there are still ways to establish direction. If the explorer has studied nature he can use that knowledge to get him home. Here are some points worth remembering.

The sun rises in the east and sets in the west.

In winter months insects hibernate in the bark on the north side of the tree.

In summer the leaves on the north side of a tree are longer and greener. They also have lighter veins than the leaves on the south side.

The north side of a tree is usually darker, softer, and wetter than the bark on the south side.

Moss is more noticeable on the north side of a tree, particularly if the tree is an elm, an oak, or an ash.

If you come across the stump of a felled tree, you will see that the bark and the growth rings are thicker on one side. This is due to the fact that less sunlight has fallen on this side of the tree. That side is therefore pointing to the north. Plants and young trees tend to bend to the south, towards the sun.

The north side of a hill is usually greener than the south side but flowers appear earlier on the southern slopes.

Spiders usually weave their webs on the south side of bushes because it is warmer on that side.

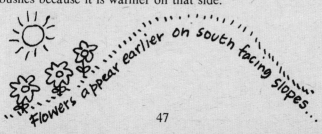

Flowers appear earlier on south facing slopes...

Going Round in Circles

Most explorers know that anyone walking without directions will usually walk in a circle. You can prove this for yourself. Blindfold a friend on a sports field and get him or her to walk in a straight line for about fifty or so paces. Even though he thinks he is walking straight he will start to move in a curve before very long.

The reason this happens is that the human body is not exactly the same on both sides. The limbs on one side of the body are different in length to those on the other side of the body. Even the muscles on each side of the body are not absolutely identical. Because the body is therefore out of balance, the muscles on one side make us move towards the left or the right – and we end up walking in a circle.

It is impossible to overcome this tendency unless you have some landmark for which you can aim or which will give you an indication of the direction in which you are walking. Remember that next time you are stranded in the desert.

Get Your Expedition in Focus

Were you disappointed with the photographic record of your last expedition? Do your friends show an enthusiastic disinterest when you get your photos from their drawer? You can avoid such post-expedition frustrations if you adopt the tips that follow.

One of the first essentials of good photography is to know your camera. This does not mean that you have to become a technical expert or own an expensive camera, but you should have at least some idea of the function of each part of the camera and you should be sufficiently at home with your equipment to be able to operate it without fumbling. The instruction book that comes with the camera should tell you all you need to know but you may find that a book on the basics of photography will prove to be a worthwhile investment.

Inside every film there is a small instruction sheet that you probably just throw away. Don't! Take a good look at that slip of paper for it contains a great deal of useful information. It will give you handy guidelines as to the shutter speed and aperture (if your camera is fitted with such refinements) to be used under various weather conditions. By making use of this information you will be well on the way to obtaining better pictures.

Were you disappointed with the photographic record of your last expedition?

Do not shake the camera...

One of the principal causes of poor expedition photography is camera shake. Most people do not realise that they move the camera as they take a photograph, then they wonder why the results are fuzzy and disappointing. To overcome camera shake when holding the camera up to your eye, press it against your cheek to hold it steady. Tuck your elbows in to gain added support. It is also a good idea to hold your breath gently for a second or so as you press the shutter release.

Camera shake can also be avoided if you squeeze the shutter release gently and if you stand firmly with your feet slightly apart. If there is a wall handy, lean against it for support, or rest your elbows on a fence or the back of a stationary hippopotamus as you take the picture. If it is at the right height, the camera can actually be placed upon some object such as a rock, the boot of a Land Rover, or the rump of a rhinoceros, to make sure that the camera is steady.

And, whatever you do, make sure the camera is level when taking the photograph or the resultant picture will appear to have been taken on the side of a mountain. Even when actually taking photographs during expeditions to the Alps the camera should be held level.

You must keep the picture simple if it is to have the

impact you desire. A photograph full of bits and pieces is confusing to the eye. The human eye is selective, it sees only what it wants or expects to see, but the camera sees everything – the primitive gas works in the background, the ancient Egyptian electricity pylons, or the native hordes watching your progress through the bush. To avoid this mass of detail try to compose your picture just as an artist would to cut out any extraneous matter. One simple way this can be done is to get closer to your subject: instead of a harbour full of fishing boats get closer and take just one or two, or get closer still and take just a net drying in the sun, and your pictures will achieve an impact they never had before.

If taking pictures of landmarks or buildings, get one or all of the expedition party into the photograph as well. But try not to pose them like statues. Make sure they are doing what they would normally be doing in that situation if the camera was not there: haggling with a stall holder in a market, asking directions from a native policeman, or simply admiring the view – anything other than looking as if they are just lumps of plasticine that happened to be there.

Do not always take a photograph from the first viewpoint you come across. Take a good look at your subject from all sides and see if you can take a picture that will be a little different and more alive than those taken by other explorers. This, however, is a rule that should be broken

The chance may never occur again . . . . . .

immediately if something happens spontaneously, when you should get it recorded on film at once for the chance may never occur again.

An impressive but simple technique is that of providing a natural frame for your picture. One way of doing this is to take the photograph through an archway, a doorway, or a window, with a portion of the arch visible on two or more sides of the picture. If taking photographs in the country, the branch of a tree or bush will provide an attractive frame that will help to add interest and depth to the photograph.

It is worthwhile carrying a notebook and pencil along with your camera to jot down brief details of each photograph you take. There is no need to write a lot, just enough to remind you when and where the picture was taken. If you take a lot of photographs during your expedition, you will be hard pressed to remember the details of each and every one of them. Your notebook, even if it gives only the place, will help to spark your memory so you can then write the details on the back of the print or in your expedition album.

As a general rule, keep the sun to your side. Do not keep it behind you as is generally advised for this will result in flat, lifeless pictures. Also, if you take pictures of your fellow explorers or of the natives with the light behind you the sun will be shining directly into their eyes. So do not

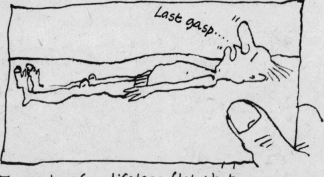

Example of a lifeless flat photo

52

be surprised if you find your subjects all have their eyes tightly closed when the prints are developed.

You may like to take your photographs so they tell the complete story of your expedition when shown in order. To do this it is worthwhile drawing up a "shooting plan" before the expedition so you do not forget to take pictures that may prove essential to your story: setting out from home, arrival at the native village, the first day on safari, and so on.

It is not expected that by following these tips you will become an expert photographer but they will help to make your expedition photographs more interesting and, as memories fade, your photos will be the only permanent reminder of an enjoyable and possibly historic adventure.

Forget all the tips if you are being chased by a crazy crocodile. Just make sure that you get away quick or it will be the crocodile and not you that takes the most interesting snap.

A Question of Weather

One of the most important things an expedition leader needs to know during the long trek is "What's the weather going to be like?" You can of course find out by listening to the radio or by telephoning special numbers to obtain the information. But if you are in the arid deserts of Bognor Regis, the telephone and the tom toms have broken down, or you simply like the idea of finding out for yourself, it is possible to become your own weather forecaster. It can also be great fun.

To find out what the weather is about to do, simply open your eyes and your mind and look at all the signs that surround you. There are many things in nature that will tell you what weather is to come. It must be admitted that these signs may not be infallible, but some work better than others. Try learning them anyway. By observing all the different signs you should be able to get a reasonable idea of what the weather is likely to do.

Spiders are particularly good weather men. If a spider shortens the threads that support its web it is a good indication that rain is due. When the spider starts to lengthen the strands once again then sunshine is on its way. Immediately before and during a rainstorm a spider will remain still on its web. If, however, you find a spider that is active while it is raining, you can be sure that the rain will not last for long. Do not try this technique with man-eating spiders found in the jungle. They are not interested in the weather – only in you!

Spiders are particularly good weather men.....

There are many weather signs associated with birds – some more reliable than others. If you see swallows or larks flying high that is a sign of good weather. Another bird to watch out for, particularly if your explorations take you near the coast, is the seagull. If you see plenty of gulls the weather should be fine. But if all the gulls have flown inland for their holidays you had better watch out, for an old rhyme says:

> Seagull, seagull, sit on the sand
> It's never good weather when you're on the land.

If you see a cat rushing round and round trying to catch its own tail it is an amusing sight. But to the dedicated explorer and weather forecaster it is also a sign that the weather is about to change. It is also said to be an indication that rain is on its way when a cat washes behind its ears. The same is not true when you see a boy washing behind his ears. That is simply a sign that his mother told him to do it.

It has long been said that a fir cone can tell you the weather to come. When bad weather is on its way, the cone closes up. It opens out again when the weather is going to be good. The same is true of daisies. They open their petals to greet the fine weather but start to close when it is likely to rain.

While you are testing these old country methods keep an eye on the sky, for that too predicts what the weather is going to be like. The old rhyme, *Red sky at night, shepherd's delight; Red sky in morning, shepherd's warning,* is remarkably accurate. So if you see a red sky in the evening it is a good indication that tomorrow's weather will be fine. If, on the other hand, there is a red sky early in the morning you can be sure that it is not going to be a very nice day. Another old method says that there is fine weather on the way if there is enough blue sky to make a pair of trousers for a sailor. Unfortunately, no-one seems to know the sailor's size!

Clouds are very good indicators of what sort of weather is on its way. Cirrus clouds, delicate feathery clouds very high in the sky, mean fine weather if they fade away. But if they thicken up you can expect rain. At a slightly lower level in the sky cirrocumulus clouds form. These consist of a layer of small flaked clouds resembling the scales of a fish. If you see this type of "mackerel sky", get the umbrella out, for it usually means there is a light shower to come. Another cirrus (hairlike) cloud is cirrostratus. This forms a greyish veil over the whole sky and is another indication that bad weather is on its way.

CIRRUS

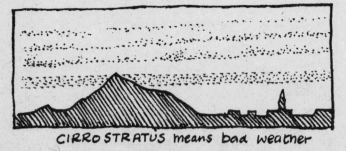

CIRROSTRATUS means bad weather

Beneath the cirrus clouds come the cumulus, which are fluffy or lumpy. Cumulonimbus clouds are large masses of lumpy clouds which often have at their peak a large lump in the shape of an anvil. If these clouds are directly above you there is no need to predict the weather – it is raining already. If they are some distance from you, watch which way they travel. If they move away, all well and good, but if they come towards you, take cover or you will get wet!

CUMULUS means good weather

The weather predicted by altocumulus clouds, which appear in whitish layers – a lumpier version of cirro-cumulus – depends upon the height at which they form. If they are rather low in the sky then once again you can expect rain. But if they are high there is a good chance that they will simply drift away and give way to fine and sunny weather.

CIRROCUMULUS or "mackerel sky"

The best clouds to see during your expedition are cumulus – especially if they are particularly white and fluffy. When you see these clouds the sun will be shining –

hooray. But if they are thick and heavy then you can expect showers – boo – with sunny intervals in between – hooray.

STRATOCUMULUS

Stratocumulus, a fluffy but thick layer of cloud, and stratus, which is also thick but not so fluffy, form fairly low in the sky. They both indicate a miserable day, probably with a fair amount of rain and drizzle. If stratocumulus forms in the evening and has a red glow then you can be certain of a fine day tomorrow. Should you see stratus clouds in the morning and they break up early in the day, then it is quite likely that the rest of the day will be fine.

Of all the signs in nature that indicate the weather there is one you can always be sure of. If you are out in the country and you see a local native sitting on a fence chewing a piece of grass, ask him what the weather is going to be like. It is more than likely that his prediction will be reasonably accurate. He listens to the weather forecast on the radio!

Bottle Barometer

A barometer is a device that gives you a forecast of changes in the weather. You can make one quite easily with a bottle and a jam jar.

The bottle should be of a size that when it is placed upside down in the jam jar the sides of the jar hold it in position. The neck of the bottle should be at least eight centimetres from the bottom of the jar.

Now pour some water into the jar. It should be about ten centimetres deep so it covers the neck of the bottle. When the weather is stormy the water level in the neck of the bottle will go down. If the water level rises, then there is good weather on the way.

For best results, the water level on a stormy day should be just touching the neck of the bottle. To achieve this it is easiest to actually make the barometer on a stormy day. Alternatively, you can make the barometer at any time and then adjust the water level on a stormy day.

Put the barometer outside and you can then use it to tell you what the weather is going to be like. When there is no water in the neck of the bottle it is going to be stormy. A slight rise indicates that there is going to be a change in the weather. As the water goes up the neck of the bottle you can be sure there is going to be fine and dry weather. But if the water level starts to drop again you had better pack your umbrella before starting your explorations.

water level in neck of bottle

Jam jar should have enough water in it to cover the neck of the bottle

Gauging the Rain

Which is the rainiest month of the year? That could be an important question in deciding when you and your party want to go away on expedition. You can find out from official records, but remote areas of the world do not keep such records. So why not discover the answer for yourself? You can if you make this rain gauge.

Put a plastic funnel upside down in a jam jar and you have a rain gauge. It is as simple as that! Put your rain gauge outside your tent and leave it there. At the end of each month measure how much water you have collected. Write the amount down in a special rain gauge measurement book. At the end of a year you will have a complete record of the rainfall for each month of the year. Now you will know which is the rainiest month!

Match Tip

Here is a way you can keep your matches dry during an expedition. Before you start out on your journey, get a candle, light it, and hold it over a shallow tin so that the wax melts into it. Before the wax solidifies, pour it from the tin and over the matches in the drawer of the matchbox. Make sure there is a large sheet of paper underneath the drawer so you do not make a mess. When the wax has cooled, the drawer can be put back into the cover, although you may have to break off some bits of excess wax before you can do this. Keep this wax-filled box of matches wrapped in a small sheet of tin foil for added protection. The foil and the wax will keep the matches dry until you need them.

To use a match you will have to dig it out of the wax. You may also find it necessary to remove some of the wax from the matchhead before it will strike – but that is much better than having wet matches that will not strike at all.

As a general rule do not take safety matches with you on an expedition. Non-safety matches are more useful because you can strike them on a wide variety of surfaces. But do be extra careful with matches of the non-safety variety. The wax coating described above will, however, make matches much safer to carry.

Non-safety matches can be struck on a wide variety of surfaces....

Fire Drill

If you plan to do your camp cooking over an open fire, please get permission from the owner of the land first. And to avoid leaving an unsightly scar on the countryside cut out a few turves and some soil where you intend to have your fire. Keep them nearby. Replace them when you leave your camp site, first making sure that the fire is well and truly out, so everything is back to normal once again.

Put stones around the outside of the area you have cut out for the fire. This will help to prevent the fire from spreading. It is also advisable to clear any dry grass, bracken, and twigs from the immediate vicinity of the fire just in case a spark should leap from the fire and catch it alight. Do not throw this dry material away. Keep it to fuel your fire.

If you are cold, move closer to the fire

brrr brrr

To build your fire, use some screwed-up paper for the centre. Do not screw the paper too tightly. Place some small twigs or bracken on top of the paper and then put some bigger twigs on top. These and some even larger twigs should be arranged in a pyramid formation for best results.

If you want a fire that will last a long time without too much attention, make a star fire. First make a fire in the normal way. When it is burning brightly, place five or six reasonably thick logs in it so that their ends radiate from the centre of the fire like the spokes of a wheel. As the centre portion of the logs burns down, all you have to do is push the other ends in towards the centre every so often to keep the fire kindled.

Pyramid fire   Star fire...

How do you light the fire? Well, you could rub two sticks together as Boy Scouts are supposed to do. You could even try rubbing two Boy Scouts together but that is not very effective either. The easiest thing to do is make sure you have a box of matches in with your camping gear so you can light the fire without fuss or bother.

It is very important that you take every precaution to prevent the risk of fire to the surrounding countryside. Within minutes, vast areas of woodland can be destroyed by a forest fire. You would not wish to have such a disaster on your conscience so guard against the risk of fire at all times.

Never light a fire near trees or bushes.

Never make a large fire. It is a waste of wood. Make a small fire. It is easier to fuel and control. If you are cold, move closer to the fire.

Camp Cooking

Cooking on safari is great fun. For some unknown reason food cooked over an open fire out in the wilds has a taste all of its own – burnt!

Cooking, like all other explorer skills should be practised first. It is, of course, fairly easy to try out cooking techniques in the luxury of your kitchen. But you will find it much more valuable to the success of your expedition if you try cooking in the garden under conditions similar to those that you will experience in your camp.

It is possible to cook full course elaborate meals over a camp fire but the recipes given on the pages that follow will be confined to meals that require very little preparation:

Jacket Potatoes
Baked potatoes make a great meal for a cold night and they are very simple to cook. Wash each potato but do not peel it, and then wrap it in some cooking foil. Now simply place the foil packages in among the ashes of the fire. Cover them with the ashes and keep the fire nice and hot.

Every so often push a fork into one or more of the packages. If the fork goes in easily the potato is ready to be eaten. Remove it from the foil (careful, it will be extremely hot), cut open the potato and pop in a large knob of butter or a lump of cheese. Delicious.

Camp cooking produces a flavour all its own..

Bangers

The easiest way to cook sausages is simply to impale a sausage on a long, sharpened stick and hold it in the fire. An alternative method is to wrap all the sausages in tin foil and pop the package into the ashes as you did for the baked potatoes. Yet a third method is to use a frying pan as you would at home. Make sure you prick the sausages first or they may explode – no doubt that is why they are known as bangers.

WARNING! HIGH EXPLOSIVE SAUSAGES

Toast

Toast is always extra nice when done over an open fire. It sometimes gets a little charred but that only seems to add to the taste. Use a long stick as you did for the sausages.

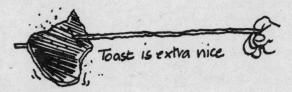

Toast is extra nice

Scrambled Eggs

Put two eggs into a small saucepan with a pinch of salt and a little pepper. Pour in a small amount of milk and place the pan on a low fire. Keep stirring and eventually the eggs will begin to solidify. When they are hot and fluffy tip them out on to some of the hot toast you have just made.

If there are several of you in the camp you can easily make a larger quantity. Allow two eggs for each person. While one person is making the scrambled eggs, a second one can be preparing the toast, and a third can be brewing up a pot of tea. That'll make a fine breakfast to start the day.

Twisters

Get a plastic bag and put into it two handfuls of self-raising flour, a pinch of salt, and two teaspoons of baking powder. Pour in a little water and twist the neck of the bag. Now squeeze the bag repeatedly until a dough is formed. Preparing the dough in a bag like this is much the easiest way to mix any ingredients when camping.

You now need some long green sticks. Remove the bark from one end and put this into the fire for a short while. Now take a lump of dough, shape it into a long sausage and wrap it around the stick. Put this in the ashes of the fire until the outside of the dough becomes golden brown.

Break open the twister of dough, put in some butter and jam, and eat it . . . Mmm.

Foiled Fish

First you must gut and clean the fish – this means taking out all the innards – and then wash it thoroughly. Now wrap it in foil and place it in the fire for ten to fifteen minutes. If you like you can even put some vegetables in the foil with it – mushrooms, chopped onions, diced carrots, whatever takes your fancy. Make a small puncture in the foil to allow steam to escape.

Soup

Soup is a very nourishing and warming food. It is also very easy to make. Simply use a dehydrated packet soup.

All you have to do is put it in a saucepan together with the recommended quantity of water and within about five minutes over the fire you have a delicious bowlful of nourishing soup.

Baked Apples

Once again this recipe makes use of cooking foil. It is such a useful commodity when camping that you should always take a roll of it with you. To bake apples, first remove the core. Fill the centre up with raisins and sugar and then wrap it in the foil. Now what do you do? That's right! You pop it in the ashes. By the time you have eaten your main meal this delightful dessert will be ready.

Camping Kebabs

Kebabs are a simple way of preparing appetising and attractive meals during an expedition. You will need some long metal skewers and the meal is so delicious it is worth buying some of these specially. But you can also make reasonable skewers with green sticks. Select some long sticks, but try not to damage the plant too much when you cut them off, and then strip off the bark. Put them near the fire for a while to dry out the sap.

What do you put on the skewer? The answer is: almost anything you fancy. You could try sausages, bacon rolls, pineapple, and pepper; steak, kidney, apple, and mushrooms; diced fish, lemon slices, and peppers; or almost any combination of these. If using meat or fish you may find it worthwhile cooking this just before putting it on the skewer as it may take too long otherwise.

Push the various pieces of food on to the skewers and then hold them over the fire, turning them frequently to prevent them from getting burnt and to heat them evenly. A forked stick pushed into the ground on either side of the fire will hold the skewers for you. Every so often rub some olive oil, melted butter or margarine over the food.

When the food is hot, use a fork to push it off the skewer and on to a plate. Do not eat it directly from the skewer, especially if you use a metal one, as it will be extremely hot.

Camper's boot stew
delicious

Doorsteps

Doorsteps are simply large sandwiches. The thickness of
the doorstep depends upon how hungry you are and how
big your mouth is. Make a sandwich in the usual way but
cut thicker slices of bread than normal. As the bread is
extra thick make the fillings extra thick also. Put in everything you can think of. Here are some ideas you can try:
lettuce, tomato, spring onions, and cucumber; beefburger,
cheese, and pickle; apple, banana, and dried fruit; or egg,
bacon, and mushrooms.

Gammon Steak

Buy a thin gammon steak from your nearest trading post.
Wrap it in foil with a slice of tinned pineapple (take it out
of the tin first). Make a couple of small holes in the foil
to let out the steam. Now put the foil parcel in the embers
of your camp fire for about five minutes.

Campers' Casserole

Chop some stewing steak, potatoes, onions, and carrots
into small cubes. Put them all in a sheet of foil and add a
knob of butter and some salt and pepper. Wrap the foil
around the food and make two or three small holes in the
top to let the steam out. Leave the foil package in the hot
embers of your camp fire for ten to fifteen minutes and you
have a tasty and warming meal. Other meats can be
used in place of the steak if preferred. Try it with different
vegetables as well.

Safari Sandwiches

For these sandwiches with a difference you need some long rolls or a French loaf. If using the loaf, cut it into pieces about fifteen centimetres (six inches) long. Cut the pieces of bread down the centre and spread a thin layer of butter or margarine on them. Now add your favourite sandwich filling. If you do not have a particular favourite you could try chopped salami with cream cheese; or tinned fish with pickled gherkins; dates and cream cheese; or baked beans with pre-cooked sausage; or sliced apples and mayonnaise.

Put the other piece of bread on top and you have made an ordinary sandwich. The difference comes when you wrap each sandwich in foil and put them in the embers of your fire for a minute or two. Eat them while they are still warm.

Doorsteps depend on the size of your mouth...

Twig It

In order to cut down on the weight you have to carry on an expedition, make as much use as possible of the countryside around you. Even if you are camping for a long period and having to wash clothes, there is no need even to carry a washing line. The clothes will dry just as well if they are draped over a bush or hung over the branch of a convenient tree. Just be careful that the branches sticking out so conveniently are not the horns of a water buffalo or something similar – or they could prove to be the horns of a dilemma for you and for your washing!

A useful towel holder can be made from three twigs. Two of the twigs must have forks in them, the third twig should be reasonably straight. The two forked twigs are pushed into the ground. The straight twig is then rested in the forks. Towels and clothes can now be draped over the straight twig to dry.

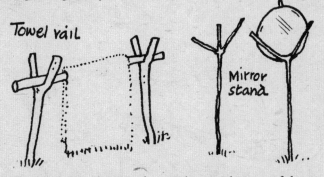

Towel rail

Mirror stand

Two forked twigs can be used to make a useful pot holder. Push one twig into the ground. Now rest the second twig on the fork of the first. A pot of water, soup, or something similar can be hung on the second twig and suspended over a fire for cooking. The fork of the second twig prevents the pot from slipping down the twig and away from the fire. If you go camping for a long period you may find it necessary to replace the second twig from time to time as it gets burnt.

Pot holder

Another way of supporting cooking pots over a fire is to use three large stones. This method is particularly suitable for a frying pan. Arrange the three stones, each of which should stand at about the same height, in a triangle. Build your fire within the triangle. You can now rest your frying pan on the three stones and cook your bacon and eggs – smashing!

Three sticks pushed into the ground make a simple but handy stand for a wash bowl.

If you can find a stick that has a three-pronged fork on it you can use it as a mirror stand. Push the stick into the ground and use the triple fork to support the mirror as shown. You will now be able to maintain a smart appearance ready for the day when the newspapermen come to interview you about your incredible exploits.

Useful bowl holder

DOG FOOD

Hang Up

To make a cup rack all you need is a twig that has several branches coming off it. Cut down each branch so that it forms a short hook. Push the twig into the ground and cups can now be hung from each of the hooks.

The same technique can be used to make a shoe holder. All you have to do is not cut the branch hooks quite so short. It is a good idea to use such a hooked twig for your shoes as they can then air out during the night while you are asleep.

Do not use the same twig for both cups and shoes. No-one wants to make a delicious cup of tea only to find that it stinks of your sweaty feet. Ugh!

Twig cup rack

On the Rack

Making a plate rack for your camp site is quite easy. First lay two sticks on the ground side by side. Now push sticks into the ground on either side of the two horizontal sticks all along their length, as shown in the illustration. When the plates have been washed they can be positioned between each pair of sticks as shown and they will drain without being in contact with the ground. The only problem is finding someone who will volunteer to do the washing up!

The plates will drain without touching the ground !

Simple Seat

To make this simple bench seat for your camp site, all you need are three logs and an axe. Cut a deep groove in two of the logs. Now rest the third log across the first two logs in the grooves so it does not fall off. Look at the drawing and you will see how simple the seat is.

If you want a better version you will also need a saw. With this method you only need one log. Saw it down the centre. Now saw one half of the log into two. Use the axe to cut a groove in each of these quarters. Now rest the half log in the grooves as before and you have a reasonably comfortable bench. It is as well to smooth down the surface of the seat before you use it or you may well get a splinter where you do not want one!

WATCH OUT FOR SPLINTERS!

Elephants' Graveyard

Whilst hacking his way through the jungle, the great African explorer Dr. Levine Stone came across a signpost pointing the way to the elephant's graveyard. For years the daring doctor had been searching for this legendary place where elephants go to die. And now at long last he had found it! But there was just one snag – the path indicated by the signpost split into several other paths. These are shown in the picture on this page. Which way should Dr. Levine Stone go to reach the elephant's graveyard?

Weapon with a Come-back

I'ts all coming back to me now....

The boomerang can be extremely dangerous...

If you ever go exploring in the Australian bush you may find it worthwhile learning how to throw a boomerang, the principal weapon of the Australian aborigine.

The main reason why a boomerang returns to the thrower is the peculiar aerodynamic shape of the boomerang. Its curved form causes it to revolve whilst in the air so that after flying in a straight line for a distance this spinning action causes it to turn in the air and return to the thrower. To help in this action the boomerang is flat on one side and rounded on the other and there is a slight twist in the wood. When the boomerang is in flight, the air presses against the rounded side which helps to cause the boomerang to turn in the air and return, provided that it has not hit anything.

To throw a boomerang, one end is held in the right hand with the other end pointed forward and slightly towards the sky. The curved side of the boomerang is on the inside, nearest to the thrower's head. When the boomerang is released the wrist and the fingers combine to give it added impetus to start the boomerang spinning.

Like all weapons, the boomerang can be extremely dangerous and care must be taken in its use.

House of Ice

If you have ever tried building a snow house like the Eskimos you will find that it is not an easy thing to do. The Eskimo people, however, who have been building snow houses for thousands of years, have it down to such a fine art that one man can build a family-sized igloo in under one hour. Every explorer should know how it is done just in case they should get stranded in the Arctic wastes. It is not really suitable for the Arabian desert, however, as the snow has a tendency to melt. Here is how Eskimos do it:

First they cut blocks from hard snow about forty centimetres square and some ten to fifteen centimetres thick. These are then arranged into a spirally ascending circular wall. Each course of the wall is built inwards slightly from the one below so that a dome-shaped house $2\frac{1}{2}$ metres high is eventually formed.

1st stage

2nd

Your finished Igloo

Made from Arctic Waste

The blocks are shaped and welded together by cutting with sharp knives. To further strengthen the walls, some Eskimos melt the surface of the internal wall for about half an hour and then let it freeze over once more. This forms a hard glaze of ice that binds the snow blocks together.

A long, low tunnel excavated in the snow or built of snow blocks forms the entrance to the igloo, and a large block of snow is used as a door. Blocks of snow are also used to form a sleeping platform and other items of furniture.

In some igloos a pane of ice is placed in the roof to provide some measure of light.

It's a Strain

To be on the safe side, all water obtained from natural sources during an expedition should be boiled before use. If you are at all doubtful about the purity of the water then boil it for at least half an hour before using it for any purpose other than washing (assuming, of course, that you do wash – and your colleagues will not be too happy if you don't!).

If the water is reasonably pure but rather muddy there are two things you can do before using it. You can collect the water in a bucket and leave it standing for a while until the mud settles on the bottom, or you can filter it. To do this simply pour the water from one container into another through a piece of cloth. If you do not have any cloth available then a bunch of grass will act as a reasonable filter.

Still Waters

If you are lost in desert regions or any other hot area where there is no water readily available, you can try making this still. Dig a deep hole. It should be at least one metre (three feet) deep – deeper if possible. Put a bucket or similar container in the bottom of the hole. Surround the bucket with freshly cut greenery if there is any available. Now place a plastic sheet, or a ground sheet, over the hole. It should extend as far into the hole as possible but it is important that it does not touch either the bucket or the greenery that surrounds it. Hold the sheeting in place at the top of the hole with some large stones. Use as many stones as you can find in order to make the area beneath the sheeting as airtight as possible.

A small stone should now be placed in the centre of the sheet, directly over the bucket.

Leave the still in place for at least one complete day. Do not disturb it until the following evening. During the day the hot sun will draw some of the moisture from the ground and from the greenery. Because of the conditions you have created this will turn into water vapour. This vapour will gather on the underside of the plastic sheeting where it will turn back into water and then drip down into the bucket.

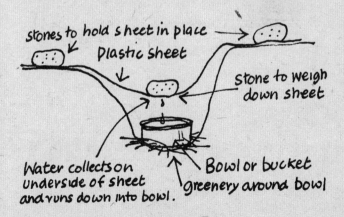

stones to hold sheet in place
Plastic sheet
Stone to weigh down sheet
Water collects on underside of sheet and runs down into bowl.
Bowl or bucket
greenery around bowl

Jungle Jokes

"The Umpabola tribe who live in the dense jungles of Borneo are vegetarian cannibals."
"That's a contradiction. How can they be vegetarian and cannibal at the same time?"
"They only eat Swedes."

What do monkeys sing at Christmas?
Jungle bells, jungle bells, jungle all the way.

What jungle animal can you never trust?
The cheetah.

What is yellow, very sweet, and swings from tree to tree?
Marzipan of the apes.

What two letters does Tarzan swing from?
I.V.

What is a cannibal's favourite food?
Baked beings.

What were Tarzan's last words?
Who greased that vine?

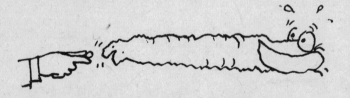

What do doctors give nervous elephants?
Trunkuillizers.

What is white and fluffy and beats its chest in a cake shop?
A meringue-utang.

Why do lions eat raw meat?
Because they don't know how to cook.

What steps should an explorer take when he is attacked by a bull rhinoceros?
Very long ones.

Who often invites his friends to dinner?
A cannibal.

How do porcupines kiss?
Very carefully.

The explorer had made friends with a tribe of cannibals. One day the chief showed him his collection of human skulls. Two of the skulls, one small and one large, were hung on poles separate from the rest. "What's so special about those two skulls?" asked the explorer. "Ah, I thought you might be interested in those," said the chief. "The big one is the skull of the famous explorer Howard I. Know." "And what about the little one?" the explorer asked. "That's the skull of Howard I. Know when he was a little boy," replied the chief.

As the explorer emerged from his tent in the Brazilian jungle he saw one of his colleagues spreading a white powder all round the camp. "What's that for?" asked the explorer. "It is to get rid of polar bears," his colleague replied. This answer rather surprised the explorer. "But there are no polar bears in the Brazilian jungle!" he exclaimed. "Which just proves how effective this powder is," replied his colleague.

Survival in the Water

All explorers should know how to swim. If you cannot swim and you wish to emulate the great explorers, go to lessons before you start on any expedition – it will be well worthwhile. But even when you can swim there may be times when you experience difficulties. It is at such times that a knowledge of survival techniques may prove to be very useful. Like all other techniques these should be practised before the time comes when you actually need them.

The first technique is that of floating, which all swimmers should be able to do. Lie back in the water so that you are looking up at the sky. Hold your head back as far as it will go without strain. Now lift your feet and legs to the surface. You will probably find that your feet will rise almost without your bidding until they poke through the surface of the water. If you now stretch out your arms on either side you should find that you can remain floating in this position for some considerable time. The secret is to keep your body as relaxed as you can.

The key to survival in all emergency situations is not to panic. This is particularly true if you are suddenly plunged into water. This may be easier said than done, of course, but your pre-expedition planning should have included some practice sessions in the local pool so you will be prepared for some of the things that could happen – especially if your local pool happens to be full of sharks.

Thrashing the water in panic and yelling frantically may help to keep the sharks away and will probably also scare the life out of the jellyfish. But it will also use up all your energy and make you more prone to drowning. As you go down for the last time you will be saying to yourself, "I wish I had taken the advice in *The Explorer's Handbook* and remained calm."

Once you are composed you can take the first of your steps to survival. This is so obvious that most people do not think of it. Check that you are out of your depth. If you have been shipwrecked out at sea or in the middle of a wide river you could think that this would be a waste of time. But you could be mistaken. You might be over a coral reef, or on a sandbank, or in an area that is much shallower than you thought.

To check the depth, first get yourself into an upright position. Give a downwards kick with both legs and push downwards with both hands to thrust your body as high out of the water as you possibly can. At the highest point of your upward thrust take a deep breath, put your hands together above your head, hold your legs together, and point your toes downward. If your feet do not touch bottom then you are out of your depth. If, however, you find that you can stand in the water it will give you a chance to look around you and consider the situation.

In your survival kit you should have some dried fruit such as raisins. If you have, your troubles are over. Just float in the water and sprinkle the dried fruit all around you. With a bit of luck the *currants* will carry you to the shore.

How to Get Into a Lifebelt

To get into a lifebelt sounds the easiest thing in the world – until you try to do it. If there is one available at your local swimming pool ask the attendant if you can practise getting into it. You may never have to use the skill you acquire but its always better to be safe than sorry.

There is a definite technique to getting into a lifebelt. If the thrower has aimed it correctly it should be floating just in front of you. If it is not, then you must get it into that position before you can go any further.

Grab the part nearest to you and push it down into the water and then away from you. This will have the effect of flipping the lifebelt completely over. If you are in the right position it will fall over your head.

Push one arm through the belt and then put the other arm through. It's easy when you know how!

Hold on to Your Clothes

Many articles of clothing can be used to keep you afloat in an emergency. First remove the article of clothing and then close all the openings, such as sleeves, trouser legs, waistband and so on that you can. This can be done by tying a few knots in strategic places. If you are wearing a belt this can be used to close the largest opening. Leave one opening free and wave the garment in the air to force as much air into the garment as possible. If you leave a narrow opening, such as a sleeve, free you can use this to blow air into the garment. Close the final opening as quickly as possible and the air in the garment will help to keep you afloat provided that you only hang on to it gently and that you do not try to climb on to it. Do not try this technique using a string vest – the holes let the air out.

The air in the garment will help to keep you afloat....

They Survived

The history of exploration is also a history of how people can survive against all odds. It is useful for all explorers to know of these stories, for one day they could find themselves in a similar situation.

In 1975, four-year-old Ben Pochee and his six-year-old cousin were stranded in the African jungle with Ben's father and the pilot of their plane that had crashed into the trees. One way that they managed to keep alive during their trek to safety was to suck dew from the leaves of trees as they had no other source of water.

John Edward Eyre explored a thousand miles of arid Australia in spite of being plagued by flies and blinded by sand and dust. At one point things got so bad that he had to slaughter his pack animals for food, and put a sponge on the ground to collect the morning dew as the water supplies ran out. To make matters worse, Eyre was in danger of being murdered by his aborigine guides – they had already killed his companion, John Baxter – but Eyre survived and his journey in 1841 has since become one of the epic stories in Australian exploration.

American Air Force Lieutenant David Steeves crashed in the High Sierras, a range of mountains in America. Conditions in the mountains were extremely cold and wintry but Steeves survived for fifty-three days as he walked to safety, in spite of the fact that he had badly sprained both ankles in the crash. He used his parachute to keep him warm as he was wearing only light summer clothing. The only equipment he had was a knife, a revolver, and some matches – but he managed to catch animals for food and he drank melted snow to keep himself alive.

Whilst exploring the Orinoco River in South America in 1800, Alexander von Humboldt and Aimé Bonpland had to endure crocodile-infested waters, impenetrable jungle, clouds of mosquitoes, and incessant rain. The rain was so torrential it ruined their food supplies and they survived for several weeks on rice, bananas and ants.

Following an aeroplane crash, seventeen-year-old Juliane Koepcke survived for ten days on her own in the Peruvian jungle. She had a wounded foot and a broken collarbone but with just a bag of sweets to sustain her she made her way to civilisation by following a river – keeping a sharp eye open for alligators and piranha fish.

Exploration Quiz

Test your knowledge of famous explorers and geography with this quiz.

1. After whom was America named?

2. Which of these explorers was first to reach the North Pole – Roald Amundsen, Robert Peary, or Robert Falcon Scott?

3. Who said, "Dr. Livingstone, I presume?"

4. Who was the first Englishman to sail around the world? Was it Francis Drake, Walter Raleigh, or Horatio Nelson?

5. After whom is Tasmania named?

6. Which of these men was the first to reach the centre of Australia – John McDouall Stewart, Charles Sturt, or Matthew Flinders?

7. Who discovered Alaska? Was it John Cabot, Ferdinand Magellan, or Vitus Bering?

8. What continent was once called "The Unknown Southern Land"?

9. After whom was the island of Tristan da Cunha named?

10. Who was the first person to fly over both the North Pole and the South Pole?

Answers on page 127

What Knots

There are several thousand different types of knots but there is no need for the explorer to know every one of them. In fact, just the five basic knots described below will be quite sufficient to enable you to cope with most situations.

Reef Knot
Take one end of the rope in each hand. Now place the left end over, across and around the right end. You have now formed a simple knot. If you now take the right end over and around the left end you have formed a reef knot. Just remember left over right, right over left and you should get it right every time. If you go wrong you will probably end up with what is known as a granny knot which is not much good for tying up anything – except possibly grannies. The reef knot, on the other hand, is quite useful for tying together two pieces of rope of the same thickness but it will not be able to take very much strain. It is also handy for tying parcels and bandages. It is doubly effective if you have a parcel that needs bandaging.

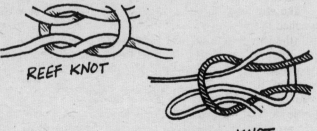

REEF KNOT

SLIP KNOT

Slip Reef
This is tied in exactly the same way as the reef knot but one end is doubled over before you start to tie the knot. If you pull the doubled-over end, the knot can be undone very quickly and easily. It is therefore quite useful for fastening tent flaps.

Clove Hitch

This comes in handy when you wish to tie something to a post. First make two loops in the rope at the centre. If you look at the drawing you will see how the loops should be formed. Place the left loop on top of the right loop. Now slip both loops over the post and pull the ends to tighten.

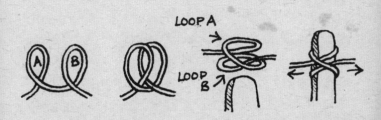

Bowline (pronounced "*bowlin*")

The bowline knot was used a great deal by sailors in the days of sailing ships. It forms a secure non-slip loop that will even support your weight (assuming of course that the rope is strong enough). It is well worth knowing just in case you need it in an emergency.

Take the *standing part* of the rope (the end that is attached to something else) in the left hand and the *running end* (the free end) in the right. Form a loop in the standing part. Now bring the running end up through the loop, around the standing part, and back into the loop again. Now pull the loop tight.

An easy way to remember how to tie this knot is to recite a little story to yourself. "A rabbit comes out of its burrow, runs around a tree, and then pops back into his hole."

Sheet Bend

A sheet bend is not, as it sounds, a way of bending sheets. It is a knot used for tying ropes together. Let us assume that one rope is thicker than the other. Take the thick rope in the left hand and bend one end of it over to form a loop. Place the end of the thin rope up through the loop you have just formed, around the doubled portion of the thick rope, and back under itself as shown in the drawing. Now pull on both ropes to tighten the knot.

It is a good idea to practise tying all these knots without looking at your hands. It is quite possible that you may one day need to tie various knots in the dark or in an awkward situation where you cannot see your hands. If this should happen to you then the practice will have proved extremely valuable.

No-one should decide to become an explorer without having some knowledge of knots. For carrying things, securing things, and even swinging through the jungle, knots are important. The knots just described will be found sufficient for most purposes but you may find it worthwhile learning some more later on.

SHEET BEND

Me Tarzan!

A Collection of Skeletons

If the prime purpose of your expedition is scientific you might like to know how to keep a record of the different types of trees you find.

During your journey, collect as many different types of leaf as you can. When you return to camp, or back to base, put the leaves into a pot of boiling water to which has been added a tablespoon of washing soda. Leave the leaves to simmer gently for about an hour. Some of your colleagues may believe that you are concocting some new type of stew but the main purpose of this exercise is to cause the flesh of the leaves to come away from the membranes.

Remove the leaves from the pot and allow them to cool. Now go over each leaf gently with a brush to remove all the flesh. Brush away from the membranes, working from the centre of the leaf and outwards.

When the leaves have been reduced to skeletons, put them into a mild bleach solution for about an hour. Rinse them in cold water and allow them to dry. They can now be stuck into an album as a scientific record of your epic journey. If you combine these skeleton leaves with the bark rubbings described on page 96 you will have a complete record of the trees you discovered.

Pressed for Time

As many expeditions have a scientific purpose it is useful for an explorer to know how to preserve some of the flowers and other plants that may be discovered. The easiest way to do this is to press them. To do this you will need some blotting paper and a book.

The flowers you wish to press should preferably be collected during the afternoon of a dry, sunny day. This is not particularly easy if your expedition is through the tropical rain forests of Borneo but you will just have to do the best you can.

Place each flower carefully between the sheets of blotting paper and then place the blotting paper inside a book. A large stone can then be placed on top of the book to press the flowers properly. If you are close to base, or when you

return there, you should pile several heavy books on top of the first. Leave the specimens in a dry room for several weeks.

For best results, the flowers should be opened out and the petals pressed flat. With some flowers you may find it necessary to take the flowers to pieces and to press sections separately.

When the flowers, leaves, and grasses have been dried out completely they can be taped into your expedition diary or displayed in your den.

The easiest way to display your specimens if you do not put them into your expedition diary is to glue them on to a sheet of card, and cover the whole display with a piece of clear, sticky-backed plastic. This will provide a washable, protective cover for your valuable specimens.

Bark Art

If one of the prime purposes of your expedition is to collect scientific data then you will need to know about bark rubbing. It is a means of recording the structure of the different types of tree that you come across during your trek through the jungle.

To take a bark rubbing all you need is a sheet of paper and a wax crayon. Some pieces of sticky tape will also prove useful. Use the tape to fix the sheet of paper to the trunk of a tree you wish to record. Now simply rub over the paper with the wax crayon. The pattern of the bark will form on the paper.

Keep all your bark rubbings in a special folder (perhaps you should call this your *log* book?), and label them, and you will eventually form an interesting and unusual record of your expedition.

Expedition Scrapbook

It is always nice to look back on successful expeditions and to recall some of the exciting and adventurous things you did. But one of the problems is that you can never remember as much as you would like. So why not make an expedition scrapbook in which you can stick photographs and perhaps write down some of your experiences? In years to come you will find it quite fascinating to look back and remember some of your most important explorations.

All you need to provide you with this expedition record is a large scrapbook or photograph album. You can buy suitable albums from most stationers but it is usually cheaper, and certainly much more fun, to make your own. The simplest way is to get an old book, something like an old encyclopedia from a jumble sale, and use that to stick things in. This has the advantage that it has ready-made covers and is properly bound. As the items you put in this scrapbook will have a thickness of their own, it is as well to go through the book first and tear out every alternate page. The pages that are left will be used to stick the photographs and other bits and pieces on. Needless to say, you should only use an old and worthless book for this purpose.

You can also make an album using several sheets of paper. For longer-lasting results a fairly stiff paper is best. Fold over the end of each sheet for about two centimetres. In the centre of each folded side punch two holes with a paper hole puncher. Alternatively, you could make the holes with a knitting needle, doing one sheet at a time – or you could put all the papers into a vice and drill the holes in the paper. If you use either of these last two methods please make sure that you only drill the holes through the papers and not through your fingers.

To hold all the papers together in book form all you have to do is tie a string or ribbon through the holes. If you like, you can make your album stronger by putting a sheet of cardboard at the front and the back to make a cover. These two sheets of card are punched in the same way as the papers. They should be slightly larger than the paper you are using.

When the album is finished you can paint or decorate the front cover.

Someone
I met
somewhere

Someone
else

Elsie

Filling the Album

It is really up to you what you put in your album – anything that will bring back memories of an important expedition. Any photographs you take during the expedition can be stuck into it. Write under each picture the date it was taken, where it is, the names of the people in it, and anything else interesting about the occasion. If you buy postcards on the upper reaches of the Amazon, or other places you visit, but never get around to sending them to anyone, they can be stuck in your album as well.

If you visit any interesting places during your expedition – game reserves, stately mud huts, lighthouses, ancient monuments – you can glue the guides and brochures into your album. If you want to, you could put the tickets in as well.

You could also draw a map on the first page of your album to show where you went and how you got there. Reserve spaces on subsequent pages to keep an expedition diary. Write down each day the most exciting, the funniest, and perhaps the most unusual thing you saw or did during the day.

There are lots of other things you can glue into your album, even pressed flowers and other specimens of native plants if you wish, so that eventually it will provide a unique and most unusual reminder of your expedition in years to come.

Me 30 Aug Africa

Me Egypt 2 Feb

My legs Oslo 13 April

Signalling for Help

If you are stranded in the outback during one of your expeditions there are several ways you can signal to passing aircraft for help. The simplest is to draw the letters SOS on the ground. You can do this with large stones or sticks or you can dig the letters in the ground. Make sure that the letters are large and as high as possible so that they can be easily seen from the air. They should be at least twenty feet (six metres) in size. It also helps if the letters cast a shadow, so, if using stones or sticks, build them high, and if digging in the ground, dig fairly deep, particularly if the area is of sand or covered in snow.

Fires are also a useful means of attracting attention. Build three bonfires, one at each corner of a large triangle. Each fire should be about a hundred yards from the others. Once they are lit put plenty of green wood and leaves on them so that they smoke a great deal.

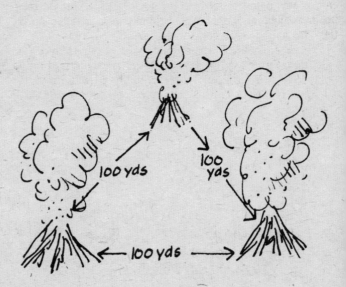

Signals on Reflection

It is always useful to have a mirror in your kit when you go exploring. In addition to enabling you to keep yourself looking clean and tidy it can be a handy signalling device in an emergency.

On a sunny day you can signal to a rescue aeroplane with this mirror. Hold the mirror up with its face between the aeroplane and the sun. Now hold your other hand up until it blocks your view of the aircraft. Tilt the mirror until the sun's reflection shines on your hand. If you now remove your hand the pilot will see a flash of light come from the ground and he will know there is someone there. Use the same sequence of signals as described for whistles on page 102 to let the pilot know that you need help.

In a real emergency, a metal badge, the polished underside of a saucepan, and even a piece of tin foil could be used to flash your emergency message.

Only transmit emergency signals when there is a real emergency. Survival is not a game. It is a very serious business. The rescue services will not be very pleased if they are called out when there is not an emergency.

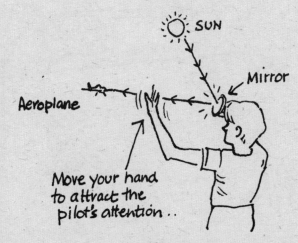

SUN

Mirror

Aeroplane

Move your hand to attract the pilot's attention..

Give a Little Whistle

When in distress, the recognised signal to give is six short blows on a whistle (you should have one in your survival kit). This is followed by a minute's silence and then six more blasts.

If a native hears you and he knows the meaning of the signal he will hurriedly convert his blowpipe into a whistle and give three blows, wait a minute, and then give three blows more.

Even if he does not know the meaning of your signal you will at least have attracted his attention. All you now have to do is to hope that he is friendly and that you do not end up in his cooking pot!

Body Language

If your expedition party is stranded and a helicopter or an aeroplane is sent out to rescue you, these are the internationally recognised signals you can use to communicate with the pilot once he can see you.

yes

Ready soon

Medical assistance needed urgently

We need mechanical parts

Pick us up

Everything alright Do not wait

Do not try to land here

Our receiver is operating

Use drop message

Land here

No

Building a Bivouac

The word "bivouac" means a temporary shelter. It is the type of shelter that you can construct in an emergency – one that will protect you for a night or two but which is not intended for use in a long-term camp.

You can use the plastic sheet from your emergency kit to provide you with a shelter. Place one end of the plastic sheet over the top of a wall and then place some large boulders on it to hold it in place. More boulders are used at the other end of the sheet to anchor it to the ground. If there is not a wall handy, build one yourself from whatever materials are to hand. Try to make the shelter as roomy as possible for you do not want to turn over in your sleep only to find that you have pulled the whole thing down on top of you.

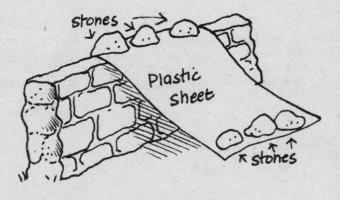

A fallen tree can often provide an emergency shelter. Place your plastic sheet over the trunk of the tree and anchor it down on each side with stones. Another method is to place fallen branches against the trunk. Alternatively, you could strip the bark from the dead tree and stack it up

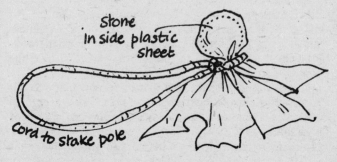

logs, or strips of bark

Fallen tree

against one side of the trunk. Fill any gaps with earth and cover the whole thing with grass or branches and you have quite a snug little shelter.

If you have a canoe handy you can make yet another bivouac. In this, the sheeting is placed over the canoe and then along the ground. The piece on the ground acts as a groundsheet. The outside edge is held down with stones as before.

There may be instances when large stones are not available to hold down the sheeting. But never fear, there is another way you can secure the sheeting. Place a small stone inside it and then tie a piece of rope around the sheeting and the stone as shown. The other end of the rope is tied to an ordinary tent peg. What, no tent pegs? Then just make some from a few twigs. It's amazing what you can do when you try.

Stone inside plastic sheet

Cord to stake pole

Snakes Alive!

There are about two hundred snakes in the world that are dangerous. That may sound a lot until you consider that there are over two thousand species that are not dangerous to man. It is therefore rather unlikely that you will encounter a dangerous snake during your expedition. It is even more unlikely that you will be attacked by a snake. Snakes will usually attack only if they are trodden on or if they think they are being attacked and they cannot get away. You cannot blame them for this – most humans would do exactly the same in similar circumstances.

To avoid being bitten by a snake all you have to do is to avoid going anywhere near a snake! A snake will not chase you – and even if it did there would be nothing to worry about for you can run a great deal faster than a snake can slither.

Make plenty of noise as you walk through the jungle and the snakes will get out of your way. If, however, you make too much noise, the local natives will hear you and you could spend the rest of the day tied to a totem pole or in a cooking pot!

Should one of your expedition party receive a snake bite, do not try cutting out the poison with a knife. It may look extremely dramatic on films but cutting the flesh will only help the poison to spread more easily. Another thing often seen in films is someone sucking the poison from the wound. Don't try this either. It is a complete waste of time.

If a member of your party is bitten by a snake the first thing to do is to take a look at the snake. Try to remember what it looks like, for an accurate description of the creature will prove essential to the doctor who is to treat the patient.

In most cases of snake bite it is important that you get the victim to a doctor as soon as possible. There are, however, a few things you can do to lessen the seriousness of the situation.

If there is clean water available you should wash the

wound. Make sure that the victim is warm and comfortable and that he does not move unnecessarily. Above all else, keep the victim calm. Very few people actually die after being bitten by a snake and it is more than likely that the creature did not inject a full dose of poison.

Before going on any expedition it as well to find out in advance what snakes you are likely to encounter and what is the best action against bites from any one of them. In the British Isles, for example, only the adder bite is dangerous – although it is seldom deadly. Snakes you are likely to encounter during expeditions to Africa or India are likely to be a little more dangerous. Perhaps the safest place to choose for your expedition is Hawaii – there aren't any snakes there, except in zoos!

Make plenty of noise when you walk through the jungle...

Snakes and Letters

The letters in each of these snakes make up the name of one of the many snakes of the world. Can you rearrange the letters to find out the name of each snake?

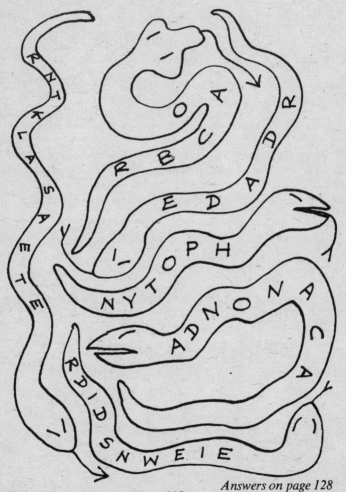

Answers on page 128

Get Sun In

A sundial is a type of clock that tells the time from the position of the sun. You can make a simple sundial of your own quite easily. All you need is a circular disc of some kind. A shallow, round box that contains processed cheese triangles is suitable, or a yoghurt carton will do quite well. You also need a straight stick.

Push the stick into the centre of the base of the box and glue it into position. Now put your sundial out in the garden on a sunny day. Once every hour go out into the garden and mark the position of the stick's shadow on the box. Against the mark put the number of the hour. Do this for every hour of daylight and you will then be able to use your sundial on subsequent days to tell you the time.

Mark the position of north on the side of the box. In the future you can use this sundial to tell the time wherever you may be. Simply point the "north" mark towards the north and the shadow of the stick will indicate the correct time.

Changes In Camp

When he camped outside the palace of the great emperor, Kublai Can't, the camp of the famous peppermint-flavoured explorer with a hole in his middle, Marco Polo, looked like the top picture. When Polo, who was always a bit of a sucker, returned, he noticed several changes in the camp. There were in fact ten changes for the camp now looked like the bottom drawing. Can you see what the ten changes were?

Answers on page 128

Who Was It?

How much do you know about famous explorers and their exploits? Test your knowledge with this quiz. Each group of clues relates to just one explorer. Can you name him in each case?

1. He made several epic voyages of discovery and exploration in the eighteenth century. He charted the complete coast of New Zealand and much of the Australian coastline as well as other parts of the world. He was killed in Hawaii in 1779.

2. He explored much of central Africa and was the first white man to travel the length of Lake Tanganyika. He discovered the Zambesi River, Victoria Falls, and Lake Nyasa. He died in 1873 whilst searching for the source of the River Nile.

3. This Norwegian explorer was the first man to reach the South Pole in 1911. In 1926 he made the first air crossing of the Arctic in the airship *Norge*. He died in a flying accident in 1928.

4. Born in Genoa in 1451, this explorer discovered much of America for Spain. His first voyage to the New World was in 1492 with the vessels *Santa Maria*, *Pinta*, and the *Nina*.

5. This Portuguese explorer led the first expedition to sail around the world in 1519 but he was killed before the voyage was completed. He named the Pacific Ocean, and the strait across the tip of South America that links the Pacific and the Atlantic is named after him.

Answers on page 128

It's a Fact

In 1642 the Dutch explorer Abel Tasman sailed all the way around the continent of Australia – but he never saw it!

In Fiji there is an ancient custom that decrees that you should smell a person's hand when you meet.

In spite of the fact that the first Spanish, English, and French vessels to reach America were all commanded by Italians (Columbus, Cabot, and Verrazano), the Italians themselves never mounted an expedition to explore the New World.

A woman of the Todas people in Southern India is required to greet a man by bowing and placing his foot to her forehead.

For eighteen months the *Fram*, the ship of the Norwegian explorer Fridtjof Nansen (1861–1930) was trapped in the Arctic ice – but Nansen had put it in this dangerous position deliberately. He thought that the drifting ice would carry him over the North Pole – it did not.

Greetings among the people of the Andaman Islands in the Indian Ocean consists of blowing upon the other person's hand.

This is a funny How-do-you-do!...

Columbus was never known by that name while he was alive. His real name was Cristoforo Colombo.

The natives of North America were called Red Indians by the early explorers because they were searching for a new route to India and because the natives often daubed their skins with reddish earth – as a result they became known as "redskins".

Although Columbus discovered and explored much of the east coast of America, he believed the lands he found to be part of Asia. It was not until after his death that it was realised this was not the case.

Some of the women of South America wear a live red and black snake around their neck as a living necklace.

It is generally believed that Columbus was the first European to land in America but the Vikings were there long before him. In about the tenth century, the Viking mariner Leif Ericsson sailed west to discover the lands of Helluland, Markland, and Vinland. It is now thought that these new lands were in fact Labrador, Nova Scotia, and New England.

If you are exploring the River Amazon in Brazil do not fall asleep. In this region there is a species of bee that delights in cutting off human hair. If you decide to have a snooze you could end up bald!

If a camel raises its tail it means he is in a bad mood. It also means that he is liable to bolt when you try to mount him. Even at the best of times camels are unpredictable and liable to bite or kick. It is a great deal safer to travel by bus!

Bottle Carrier

Here is a handy way to carry a bottle or a jar when out exploring. It will work with any bottle that has a lip round the neck. If you use several of these special ties you can carry quite a number of bottles in one hand very easily.

Fold a length of string in half. Take the centre of the string and fold it inwards to form two loops as shown in the first drawing.

Take the inner string of each of these loops and twist them twice around each other. The string should now look like the third drawing.

Now push the right hand string over the bottom of the main (double) loop and through the central twist as shown by the arrow in the third drawing and you should end up with the string like that in the fourth drawing.

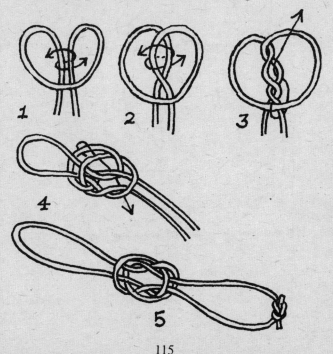

Fold the top loop at the back downwards, following the arrow in the fourth drawing, and the knot is finished. Tie the two loose ends together.

Now put the neck of the bottle into the centre of the knot and pull tight.

Penknife Candle Holder

A penknife can make a useful candle holder. Simply push the point of the main blade upside down into a tree trunk or into a stick pushed into the ground. Open the second blade so that it is pointing upwards. Now impale the candle on the point of this vertical blade and the knife will hold the candle for as long as you require.

Chopsticks

Most people think that eating with a knife and fork is the most usual way in the world. But you, as an intrepid explorer, will know that this is just not true. You will know that more people in the world use other means to tackle their food. About 900 million people use a knife and fork, some 850 million use chopsticks, and at least 750 million use only their fingers.

It is more than likely that you have been trained to use a knife and fork, and you probably do not need any training to know how to eat with your fingers. But chopsticks are not quite so easy. Any explorer who wishes to explore eastern countries should know how to use chopsticks – it is not so difficult as you may imagine.

Assuming that you are right-handed, you first have to place one chopstick in the thumb crotch of the right hand. The narrow end of the chopstick should rest on your little finger. Now place the third finger on top of the stick. Place the second stick between the first and second fingers and hold it further up between the thumb and forefinger.

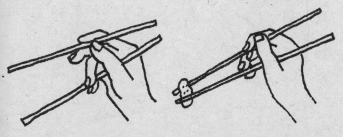

With a bit of practice you will find that you can move the upper chopstick up and down whilst keeping the lower one still. When using this technique to pick up food, try to keep the ends of the sticks at the same length. And do not open the sticks too wide or you may drop them and the food you are holding into your lap. It may seem a bit awkward at first, unless you are an oriental explorer, but with a little practice you will soon get the hang of it.

Lost Countries

Explorers are always seeking to discover new lands. See how many established countries you can discover hidden in the grid below. They may be written forwards or backwards and may be positioned horizontally, vertically, or diagonally.

```
P C A N A D A C A S
O U H O Z N I P O L
R B P I R A D Y O N
T A A E N L N I L D
U B U R M A I R A N
G S O A M E R I C A
A R P R A Z A T N L
L R E A N W P A O R
A G R S T E P L R E
T S U P E N O Y W Z
I L A A I T L R A T
B O L I V I A A Y I
E M S N O R N E O W
T A E N N E D E W S
```

Hints and Tips

If your food supplies include easily squashed fruits, pack them in egg cartons and they are less likely to become mushed up.

Milk can be kept cool on the camp site by placing the bottles in a bowl of cold water and covering them with a cloth, the ends of which are left in the water.

It is more convenient to take powdered milk for your expedition instead of carrying bottles or other liquid containers.

Save potato peelings and orange peel while you are in camp. Keep them in a dry place and they will make excellent fire lighting material.

Newspaper stuffed into wet boots or shoes will help to dry them out.

Prick eggs at the pointed end before boiling them and they will not crack during cooking.

If plastic containers start to leak, the holes can often be sealed by applying heat so that the plastic melts over the hole.

Dandelion leaves can be used in your camp cooking. Pick the young leaves and boil them in salted water.

If a bee flies into your tent the easiest way to get rid of it is to hold a flower near it. When the bee settles on the flower you can take it outside without any fuss.

Keep a few coins in your emergency kit. They may prove useful for telephoning friends and relatives when you get back to civilisation.

Strips of sellotape put along both sides of the folds of maps will give the maps a longer life.

Take some postage stamps with you when you go exploring if you intend writing to anyone. There may not be a Post Office available out in the wilds.

Before you start cooking, rub a thick layer of soap on the outside of your pots and pans. This will make them much easier to clean when the cooking is over. It is not recommended that you do this on the inside of the pans unless you like soapy food.

Hand Signals

In the days when the Red Indians were the only human inhabitants of North America, they used sign language to communicate with people from other tribes.

Explorers will find a knowledge of this sign language useful. If your camp is surrounded by wild animals you will be able to communicate with other members of your party without the animals being able to locate your position by the sound of your voice. This sign language can also prove to be a useful means of communicating with friendly natives – especially if they happen to be Red Indians.

Here are some words and their appropriate signs:

ANGER—Put closed right fist against the forehead and then move it around in a circle.

AUTUMN—Extend the right hand upwards with the fingers spread to represent a tree. Place the left hand below the right and then move it downwards with a waving action to depict falling leaves.

BAD—Hold the closed right fist against the heart. Now move the hand forwards, downwards, and outwards as you open the hand. The movement should look as if you have thrown something down to the right.

BOOK—Hold the hands together palms upward as if they formed an open book.

BRAVE—A clenched fist held against the breast.

BUFFALO—Hold the hands against your temples and crook the index fingers up to represent horns.

DANGER—Touch the top of the thumb with the tip of the forefinger to form the shape of the letter O and point towards the danger spot.

DANGEROUS—Point the right index finger forwards and then move it down in a semi-circular motion until it points to the ground.

ESCAPE—Cross the wrists with the hands closed, and then separate the hands by moving them to the left and to the right.

CRY—Point the index fingers to the inner parts of the eyes and then move them both downwards to indicate running tears.

CRY

EVERYONE—Hold right hand, palm outwards, at shoulder height with all the fingers outstretched.

EVIL—Use the same sign as for "bad".

EYES—Use the right index finger to touch each side of the nose.

FIGHT—Clench the fists and move them backwards and forwards as if boxing.

FINISHED—Brush the hands together.

FRIEND—Hold the first and second fingers together pointing upwards, with the rest of the hand closed, at chest height. Move the hand up to shoulder height.

HEAR—Hold cupped hand to one ear.

HELLO (HOW)—Hold the right hand palm outwards at shoulder height and then make one small semi-circular movement up and out to the right.

LOVE—Cross both hands over the chest.

GOOD

GOOD—Hold the right hand palm uppermost against the chest in the region of the heart.

HORSE — Hold the outstretched left hand between the index and second fingers of the right hand. This is to indicate a rider on horseback.

HORSE

MAN—Hold one finger up.

ME—Point index finger towards yourself.

PLANT—Place right fist on top of left fist and then move them downwards.

QUIET—Hold the right hand palm downward and move the hand downwards a couple of times.

RAIN—Both hands are held in front of the body, palms towards the body, with the fingers pointing to the ground. The fingers thus represent falling rain.

SEE—Hold the partly closed hand against the side of the face and point the first and second fingers forward.

SIT DOWN—Use the same sign as for "plant".

SLEEP—Cradle your head in both hands.

TRUE—Hold the right hand level with the right shoulder and then point the first and second fingers down towards the heart.

WOLF

WOLF—Two outstretched fingers pointing upward.

YOU—Point index finger at the person concerned.

And So To Bed

It is very nice to have a comfortable folding camp bed during your explorations in the wilds. But you try carrying it around with you for a few days and you will wish that you had not bothered. A simple bed can be made just by scooping a hole in the ground to accommodate your hips. You can if you like just sleep on the ground (with a ground sheet under you, of course) but the ground can be very hard and this simple hollow makes sleeping that little bit easier.

To make this bed even more comfortable you can pile some dry bracken over the sleeping area. It makes quite an effective mattress.

Another thing a lot of explorers carry is a sleeping bag. But it is also possible to make a sleeping bag with just two blankets. Lay one blanket on the ground. Now fold the second blanket in half and place it in the centre of the first blanket. Now fold the bottom of the second blanket up to form a bag. Finally fold the other half of the first blanket over. If you now turn the whole lot over you have quite a good sleeping bag. Your weight will hold the blankets in position.

There is also no need to pack a pillow. Simply place your shoes together where the pillow should be. Then fold your clothes and lay them on top of the shoes. It makes a reasonable pillow provided that your feet do not smell.

Simply place your shoes together
where your pillow should be

EXPLORING ENIGMAS

The Two Explorers. They are husband and wife.

The Long Walk. He was back at the North Pole.

Burial Party. Neither. Survivors are not usually buried!

Polar Bears and Penguins. Because polar bears live in the Arctic and penguins live in the Antarctic.

The Chase. Only halfway. After that point they are running out of the jungle.

ELEPHANTS' GRAVEYARD

Did you find the route?

EXPLORATION QUIZ

1. Amerigo Vespucci (1454–1512) who claimed to have discovered America. This claim has since been proved false although he did explore much of the South American coast; 2. Robert Edwin Peary (1856–1920) on 6th April, 1909; 3. Henry Morton Stanley (1841–1904) when he found David Livingstone on the east coast of Lake Tanganyika in November, 1871; 4. Francis Drake (c1540–1596). He set out from Plymouth on 6th April, 1577 and arrived back home on 26th September, 1580; 5. The Dutch navigator Abel Janszoon Tasman (1603–1659) in 1642. He called it Van Diemen's Land after the Governor of the Dutch East Indies, but in 1853 the British renamed it Tasmania in honour of its discoverer; 6. John McDouall Stewart (1815–1856); 7. Alaska was discovered by the Danish navigator Vitus Jonassen Bering (1680–1741); 8. The "Unknown Southern Land" (Terra Australis Incognita) was the name given to a continent believed to exist in the South Seas. It was not until James Cook discovered it during his epic voyage of 1768–1771 that its existence was proved. Today the continent is called Australia; 9. This group of islands in the South Atlantic was named after the Portuguese navigator Tristan da Cunha who discovered them in 1506; 10. Richard Evelyn Byrd (1888–1957), an American naval officer, was the first person to fly over both the Poles (North Pole in 1926 and the South Pole in 1929).

SNAKES AND LETTERS

1. Cobra; 2. Adder; 3. Anaconda; 4. Rattlesnake;
5. Python; 6. Sidewinder.

CHANGES IN CAMP

There is one less circle on the tent in the background; part of
the soldier's right ear is missing; the horse has one less piece
of fringe on its bridle; there are only two ribs in the foreground; a pennant is missing from the tent on the right; the
soldier has only one row of studs on his breastplate; the
horse has lost part of its right ear; a circle is missing from the
tent in the foreground; part of the horse's mane is missing;
part of the soldier's right leg has been left out.

WHO WAS IT?

1. James Cook (1728–1779); 2. David Livingstone (1813–
1873); 3. Roald Amundsen (1872–1928); 4. Christopher
Columbus (1451–1506); 5. Ferdinand Magellan (1480–
1521).

LOST COUNTRIES

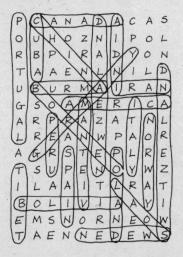